Gerstein

A Full-Length Play in Two Acts

PAUL D. PATTON

Integratio Press
Pasco, Washington

GERSTEIN

Copyright © 2023 by Paul D. Patton. All rights reserved. This publication is also subject to royalty. Except for brief quotations in critical publications or reviews, no part of this book may be reproduced in any manner without prior written permission from the publisher. Write: Permissions, Integratio Press, 11503 Easton Dr., Pasco WA, 99301.

An Imprint of Christianity and Communication Studies Network
11503 Easton Dr.
Pasco, WA 99301

www.theccsn.com

Cover design: Katie Dennison and Carol O'Callaghan
Interior design: Mary Bryant
Image: Adobe Stock and Depositphotos

paperback isbn: 978-0-9991463-9-2
ebook isbn: 978-1-959685-02-9

Trinity House is a Division of Integratio Press

Library of Congress Control Number: 2023931213

Acknowledgements

I AM INDEBTED to Pierre Joffroy's biography of Kurt Gerstein, *A Spy for God: The Ordeal of Kurt Gerstein*, translated by Norman Denny (New York: Helen and Kurt Wolf, 1970); to Henri Roques' *The 'Confessions' of Kurt Gerstein* (Costa Mesa, CA: Institute for Historical Review, 1989); to Saul Friedlander's *Kurt Gerstein: The Ambiguity of Good* (New York: Alfred A. Knopf, 1969). Thanks also to my friend and colleague, Joe Frost, who directed the premiere offering of *Gerstein* at Belhaven University in the fall of 2008. I am also indebted to the guidance of Professor Steve Smiley of Spring Arbor University for helping me over fifty years ago in my studies of the Confessing Church in Germany.

About the Author

PAUL PATTON (PhD, Regent University) is Professor Emeritus of Communication and Theater at Spring Arbor University in Michigan. It was while pastoring at Trinity Church in Livonia, Michigan, that he founded Trinity House Theater in 1981. He is the author of over 30 produced stage plays, radio plays, and performance essays. He is contributing author to the books, *Understanding Evangelical Media* (IVP), *Evangelical Christians and Popular Culture* (Praeger), and *Prophetic Critique and Popular Culture* (Peter Lang), and co-author of *Prophetically (In)Correct: A Christian Introduction to Media Criticism* (Brazos Press), and the newly published, *Everyday Sabbath: How to Lead Your Dance with Media and Technology in Mindful and Sacred Ways* (Cascade Books).

Author's Note

I FIRST BECAME INTRIGUED by the Gerstein saga when a friend of mine in Virginia handed me Pierre Joffroy's biography of Gerstein that he'd picked up from the "discard" table at William and Mary's library in Williamsburg. That was twenty-five years ago. What drew me to the story at first was how it forced me, and hopefully the audience, to push out of the convenient constraints of our understanding of the providence of God. Pondering Gerstein's story is to wander through the sometimes dis-easing depths of the book of Ecclesiastes. I'm hoping that the story of Gerstein allows for some of the same redemptive provocation.

I was also intrigued by Kurt Gerstein's depth of interiority, his engagement with biblical texts (which he quoted often), and his engagement with his "alter ego," Soren Kierkegaard (SK), whom biographer Joffroy notes Gerstein quoted extensively. Joffroy's biography of Gerstein is titled *A Spy for God*, a direct reference to Kierkegaard's well-known self-description.

I am hoping the reader notes the purposefully Brechtian style of this work—excessive use of narrators, various media forms, minimalist set, extensive use of light. I felt it was a necessary choice for such an epic story and a style appropriately German.

All quotations in dialogue are taken from other sources covering the life of Kurt Gerstein, mostly from Pierre Joffroy's biography, *A Spy for God*.

Historical Note

(Taken from the program of the play's premiere at Belhaven College in October 2008, directed by Joseph Frost)

KURT GERSTEIN has become widely known as the *SS officer with a conscience*. After his surrender to French authorities, Gerstein wrote a report in which he recounted his eye-witness experience of the operations of the Nazi extermination camps and other information he had obtained. In addition to being one of the first testimonies concerning the heart of Nazi workings, it also proved one of the most vital. Despite great opposition, his conviction that he must pursue any end to stop the Nazis remained strong. The beginning of a letter to a friend was found among his papers before he was transferred to prison in France:

"Dear friend Ubbink,
You are one of the first to whom I shall send greetings. Let me congratulate you from the bottom of my heart on the liberation of your country from our brood of vipers and criminals. However dark our fate may now be, those terrible people could not be allowed to sin. Ask your people if, now at least, they believe what went on in (Belzec), etc. I thank God that I did everything in my power to cut through this abscess on the body of humanity."

Under the name Gastein, Gerstein was buried in the Thiais cemetery, although his grave was within a section that was razed in 1956. On June 6, 1950, SS Obersturmbannführer Dr. W. Pfannenstiel verified the basic facts of Gerstein's report before the land-court of Darmstadt in the Federal Republic of Germany. On August 17, 1950, Gerstein was declared a Nazi offender by a denazification court in Tübingen, which posthumously condemned him:

"Taking into account the extenuating circumstances noted the court has not included the accused among the main criminals but has placed him among the 'tainted.' ..."

Gerstein's wife, with the help of Baron von Otter and other significant friends, obtained a pardon for her husband by the Premier of Baden-Württemberg on January 20, 1955.

Sources:
United States Holocaust Memorial Museum
www.ushmm.org/wlc/article.php?lang=en&moduleId=10005840
www.gerstein.dk/aftermath.htm
www.annefrank.dk/gerstein/new_page_4a.htm

Cast of Characters

Young Kurt Gerstein	10-13 years old, can be played by the adult Kurt Gerstein
Kurt Gerstein	Anywhere from young adult to middle-aged, studious, but also a goof-ball who loved to make the young people laugh
Regina	Young Kurt Gerstein's caregiver and guardian, matronly, even saintly
SK	This is Soren Kierkegaard, a diminutive, almost frail man
Elfriede	Kurt's wife, passionate, caring
Rehling	Pastor friend of Gerstein
Various Ensemble roles	
Mining Official	
Gestapo Interrogator	
Sergeant Robert Weigelt	Training instructor for Waffen SS
Helmut Franz	Friend of Kurt's who is wounded in battle
Wirth	Nazi commander of the death camp
Ludwig Gerstein	Kurt's father

Act One

STREAMS OF WHITE LIGHT, scorching, naked, nearly blinding, flood the STAGE, back-dropped in a wall of crimson red.

A diminutive, almost frail man arrives, as if from nowhere. His hair is tossed every which way—this is SOREN KIERKEGAARD, SK, whose thoughts possessed Kurt Gerstein (Gerstein biographer Pierre Joffroy reports that Gerstein quoted SK extensively, as extensively as he quoted from the Bible). SK lights the candles of a candelabrum placed DOWN CENTER.

SK stays to watch the scene unfold, unnoticed, but providing subsequent narration.

REGINA, matronly, sturdy, *intoxicated* by the sanctuary's holy presence, pulls a young boy, KURT GERSTEIN (can be played by adult), DOWN CENTER to the candelabra burning on the floor. SHE stops, HE crashes into her—

KURT
Regina, Regina, you pull me too hard, too fast!

REGINA
(Laughs)
Little Kurt Gerstein, you must always be pulled hard, pulled quickly into the sanctuary God provides us.

> SHE looks up and around, awestruck in the grandeur of the Presence. Rapturous, she extends her arms, lifts them to the heavens in exaltation.

REGINA (cont'd)

The heavens declare His handiwork; our hearts whisper the truth of His presence.

> KURT has wandered closer to the candles, eyes locked into the chorus of flame, closer, closer. HE reaches out his hand, drawn to touch the flame. REGINA, enraptured, does not see him.

REGINA (cont'd)

Our lives before His face and fire—Kurt, the prayers of the saints, the intercession of the Savior, the comfort of His mother!

> KURT moves, closer still, hand above the flame, face transfixed, staring into it.

REGINA (cont'd)

Be consumed by the fire of His presence. Fill your nostrils with His glory. Run to the sanctuary of God; nowhere to flee from His holy gaze.

KURT

But this is the third one this morning, Regina.

REGINA

Fortified in His bosom, drenched in the dew of God's refreshment, lost in His embrace!

KURT

A boy must have time to live elsewhere.

> HIS hand is just above the flame. SHE sees HIM.

REGINA

(Calling out)
The flame is not for burning your hand. It's the prayers of the saints, the prayers of the saints.

> KURT wets his fingers, starts to extinguish each flame.

REGINA (cont'd)
Kurt, stop it!

KURT
Do the prayers stop when the light is extinguished?

REGINA
If you don't stop, I'm getting Father Martin.

KURT
And if he won't come?

REGINA
You will go home, no more adventures with me for the day.

KURT
Maybe the fire is the adventure meant for me today.

REGINA
Father Martin!

KURT
Regina, I was born for adventure.

REGINA
You were made for holy moments, not finding fun and games by God's altar.
>	HE extinguishes the last candle.

REGINA (cont'd)
Kurt Gerstein!
>	OVERHEAD LIGHTS DIM. FATHER MARTIN enters, clown nose, attempting to juggle, but fails comically. REGINA laughs.

REGINA (cont'd)
It is Father Martin; he likes to make the children laugh.

> KURT just stares inquisitively, not giving in.
>
> KURT picks up the candelabra and slowly exits.

REGINA (cont'd)
Kurt Erich, put it back!

FATHER MARTIN
Maybe he's gone to light it, Regina. Believe me, Kurt is perfectly fine.
> KURT is gone.

REGINA
He now tells me that he doesn't like it when I call him Kurt. He wants to be called Kurt Erich.

FATHER MARTIN
His given name?

REGINA
He gave Erich to himself. The boy resented having only one. He says Kurt dreams and Erich weeps. Neither of them laughs, Father.
> SHE turns, notices KURT offstage—

FATHER MARTIN
He is too young to not laugh.

REGINA
It's time to go home to your papa. Hurry!

KURT
>(Offstage)

But I want to stay here!

REGINA
Suddenly, you want to stay here; it is too late for staying.
>(Exiting)

We must go, your papa will be angry.

KURT

He is always angry.

>THEY have exited.

SK

>(To audience, as narrator)

What of visions that will not go away, voices that persist, refusing to be stilled? He did not ask for them. They were birthed unannounced in his tiny soul as a boy too young to house such passions. He never knew enough to be thankful for them, never sure that they weren't his bridges to insanity. But nothing was easy for Kurt Gerstein, a just man among the Gentiles, one described as a name that "deserves to be remembered in history as that of a lofty, tormented conscience." But why should tormented consciences be remembered? I ask only as another tormented conscience from the century preceding his, seeing that Kurt Gerstein would lock me, Soren Kierkegaard, in his mind as what you would come to call his "alter ego."

>An *adolescent* KURT and REGINA reenter; REGINA is holding a lit candle.

REGINA

>(Calling back to a trailing KURT)

Hurry or we will miss the sunrise. Boys of thirteen shouldn't be wishing they were sleeping.

KURT

It's too early, Regina.

>CHURCH BELLS are RINGING.

REGINA

Listen to the bells, the Easter bells!

KURT

>(Reluctantly)

It is never as easy as Easter.

REGINA
What?

KURT
Rich men don't give to the poor; lepers aren't embraced by the healthy just because our Lord rose from the grave.

REGINA
(Dismissing)
Such melancholy, Kurt Erich.

KURT
Enthusiasms for resurrections die just like everything else.

A short PAUSE, REGINA turns to KURT, stunned.

REGINA
What did you just say?

KURT
Enthusiasms for resurrections die just like everything else.

REGINA
(Something has snapped in her)
What do you mean? I don't know what you mean; you don't know what you mean. You are pressing too hard on things that will not move, Kurt Erich Gerstein!

KURT turns to look at her, unmoved. HE exits.
CHURCH BELLS FADE.

SK
His business would become the digging up of the earth's minerals, Kurt Gerstein a mining engineer by profession. But what he really sought to uncover was the stamp of God in the face of evil absurdities. And this boy who became a man would witness the sacrifice of Isaac a million times over, wrestle with the Archangel, and find inextricable combinations of doubt and faith, fury and resolve.

Adult KURT reenters, wearing a mining helmet. HE is talking to another MINER.

REGINA

(To audience, as narrator)
As the family maid and nanny, I knew—even when Kurt was a toddler—there was little peace with him. I always wondered where his life would go. The pounding in his heart warned him to tell others of a day of reckoning, long before the landscape would be filled with swastikas. It seemed Kurt Gerstein heard nothing but cries for help.

KURT

"The miner always carries his shroud with him." We must not forget our life one moment from disaster is the same above or beneath the earth.

MINER

I'd rather forget!

KURT

Of course, we'd all prefer the fantasy of constant dessert.
MINING OFFICIAL enters, sees KURT.

MINING OFFICIAL

There you are Gerstein. Our lost and eccentric shepherd is found talking to a Polack. You're lucky that we like you and decided to hold up further blasting until you were found. Your round shouldn't have taken ninety minutes. You are an engineer, not a minister. But I know what the boss will say: "Gerstein is good for wherever he is." Do you have him fooled?
KURT pats the MINER on the back, the MINER exits.

MINING OFFICIAL (cont'd)

I will tell him you were spending your time treating a Polack as though he was God.

KURT

"So he was. At that moment."

MINING OFFICIAL

Is this another sermon, Reverend Gerstein?

KURT

What is it our Lord said about—

MINING OFFICIAL

"As you've done it to the least of these, you've done it unto me."

KURT

How did you know my text for this moment?

MINING OFFICIAL

Kurt Gerstein, what other text have you mentioned in the last few weeks? You've only cited sheep and goats—the naked, the hungry, the prisoner . . . the miner.

KURT

"Christ in you," Helmut Schulz (*the official's name*)—

MINING OFFICIAL

"The hope of glory," I know, I know—would that you'd let me forget.

KURT

"The miner always carries his shroud with him." We must not forget our life one moment from disaster is the same above or beneath the earth.

MINING OFFICIAL

I'll tell the boss you remain busy turning mine shafts into sanctuaries.

KURT

Are you and the children coming to dinner tomorrow?

MINING OFFICIAL
If I told them no, they'd turn into an angry mob. They love you more than they love me. It's scandalous.

KURT
It's the candy in my pockets.
> KURT tosses a candy to the MINING OFFICIAL

KURT (cont'd)
That is the scandal. We're all waiting for a treat, aren't we?

SK
Above the earth, it was the young that he poured himself into. A youth leader of legendary status, hundreds of adolescents would testify of his devotion, of his "ability to recognize their true status as human beings. Usually, such recognitions are withheld until, the flurry of youth abating, they have lost their ability to change the world." Yet Kurt Gerstein was able to tell them with great passion that they *must* change it. They must change it. So how does one describe the enthusiasm he engendered in those children? One summer all two hundred and seventy teenagers of a youth camp celebrated his birthday by staging a triumphal dance that went on for half-hour shouting, "Vati! Vati!" until finally, they carried him on their shoulders around the camp.

REGINA
He also spent money for parties, for bus rides and excursions on boats. He even paid tuition for education of the very poor children. He turned a run-down farm into a youth center. Kurt was always ready to listen, always ready to remind his youngsters of the Holy Ghost that longed to indwell them. He was always looking for new things to offer, new ways to respond to cries for help—for extinguishing fires and, when necessary, starting them.

SK
His list of eccentricities was never ending, with neither clothing nor categories ever fitting him well.

KURT

But this is not different than anyone who keeps fighting against being herded.

REGINA

Does the normal adult buy a sports car, overlooking the fact that he has not learned to drive?

KURT

I practiced and I practiced, and, eventually, my passengers stopped being afraid. All of them liked my car.

REGINA

Does the normal adult buy the most expensive suits and wear them till they are in shreds?

KURT

Buying good suits allows you to put off the tedium of buying suits.

REGINA

And does the normal adult lose his wallet and five minutes later forget that he lost his wallet?

KURT

Sometimes there are things more important than finding your wallet!

REGINA

And does the normal adult spend a whole summer looking for shorts that "aren't short?"

KURT

My legs are ugly.

SK

Kurt Gerstein joined the National Socialist Party in 1933. He was a German attracted to a movement that sought to address the injustices of Versailles.

    KURT walks off the STAGE and into the HOUSE.

SLIDE ONE: 30 January 1935 a racist and pagan drama by Edmund Kiss, entitled Wittekind was presented at the Municipal Theatre in Hagen, Germany.

KURT
> (While walking with FRIEND)

I heard that some Catholics formally demonstrated against this play on its opening night. A good Nazi play, I'm told.
> KURT and FRIEND are walking through the HOUSE toward their seat.

FRIEND
A first for me.

KURT
A good Nazi play must mean it is replete with "Heil, Hitlers."

FRIEND
Nothing more, Kurt?

KURT
I expect little artistic subtlety from us Nazis.
> THEY find their seat.

SLIDE TWO: Wittekind, Duke of Saxony

WITTEKIND
Certainly the Man of Nazareth is a convenient God. You may be a villain all your life, but if at the end you repent, grace and consolation are assured you. Is that not so, Sir Chamberlain? . . . Lurking behind the quarrelsome Germans I always see a cassock. Will Germany be forever plunged in a bloodbath in the name of this foreigner you call God?

SLIDE THREE: Albion, Duke of Verden

ALBION

(Can be played by the same actor playing Wittekind.) "We have no use for a Savior who can only whine instead of suffering in silence like a hero. We Germans . . ."

KURT

(SCREAMS from HIS seat) We have had enough! Shame! We shall not allow our faith to be publicly insulted without protest! I am not ashamed of the gospel of Christ! It is the power of God unto salvation, to the Jew first, but also to the Gentile! Our Lord also warned us that if we deny Him, He will deny us before His Father! How dare we sit on our hands in the midst of such blasphemies! This is an insult to the greater sensibilities of the German people, whose forefathers—

SEVERAL "BROWN SHIRTS" with swastika armbands converge on KURT, SCREAMING ABUSE, begin to beat HIM, and drag HIM out of the auditorium.

REGINA

He left two of his teeth there that night while he was ushered off to jail as a political prisoner and enemy of the fatherland. He would remain imprisoned, unsure of his fate, only to be freed weeks later. Still he was unrepentant.

SLIDE FOUR: Pastor Kurt Rehling, minister in Hagen, Germany. Friend of Kurt Gerstein.

REHLING

In 1932, when several Nazis were condemned to death for murdering a communist, Hitler sent an outlandish telegram to the German chancellor, Von Papen—

KURT enters, mockingly impersonating Hitler.

KURT

"Herr Von Papen, I do not accept your blood-thirsty objectivity!"

REHLING

But, Kurt, this is an alarm signal. "It means that the Christians can no longer come to terms with the Nazis. It is an open invitation, join our Party, think as we do, and you can commit any crime with impunity."

KURT

I am no less alarmed than you. But what nation of the world hasn't distorted justice for their political purposes? Perhaps the best way to prevent such evil abuses is to join the Party and fight from the inside.

REHLING

What?!

KURT

Join them and fight from the inside!

REHLING

You're a fool! Are you haughty enough to think you can sanctify that cesspool? "You are only a drop of water; the Party is the desert that devours drops of water." Besides, how can you praise the Lord, the God of Abraham, Isaac, and Jacob and "Heil, Hitler!" You are a fool, Kurt Gerstein; and please don't say—

REHLING/KURT

(Simultaneously)
I am a fool for Christ!

KURT

Perhaps it is the foolishness of the cross that bids me to pick it up in the midst of the beast!

REHLING

And wear the swastika at your jugular vein!?

KURT

Then it would be blood spilt in the name of redemption! To the gates of hell for the Cross!

REHLING

You are confusing—(your crosses)

KURT

(Cutting REHLING off)
To the gates of hell with the cross!
> (He quotes long portions of Psalm 139, over the objections of REHLING)

"O Lord, Thou hast searched me, and known me. Thou knowest my downsitting and mine uprising, Thou understandest my thought afar off. . . . Whither shall I go from Thy spirit? Or whither shall I flee from Thy presence?"

REHLING

The Lord has withdrawn His presence many times—

KURT

> (Overtaking REHLING)

"If I ascend up into heaven, Thou art there; if I make my bed in hell, behold, Thou art there!"

REHLING

> (Frustrated)

And so in May of 1933 you joined the Nazi Party.

KURT

> (Standing to attention)

Membership number 2,136,174!

REGINA

And as a Nazi party member, he made Protestant opposition to the party his personal affair. Kurt Erich was trained as a mining engineer, so early on he was given the responsibility of organizing a

REGINA (cont'd)
conference of German miners. He attacked his duty with mischievous glee. With each mailed invitation it amused him to include a homemade sticker to be attached to the train window of all conferees:

SLIDE FIVE: Train compartment reserved for travelers accompanied by mad dogs

KURT
It was a joke, a harmless—

GESTAPO INTERROGATOR
    (Entering, holding sticker, reading)
Train compartment reserved for travelers accompanied by mad dogs . . .

KURT
Ha-ha, I thought it was funny.

GESTAPO INTERROGATOR
It is nothing but mockery of party members who ride the trains.

KURT
Not to all train passengers who happen to be party members, just those traveling to the conference of mining engineers, who happen to be party members, who happen to be accompanied by mad dogs.

GESTAPO INTERROGATOR
Pardon me, Party Member
    (HE looks at membership card)
2,136,174, but I neither see nor hear anyone in the German universe laughing.

KURT
It is a joke costing me my freedom, I suppose?

GESTAPO INTERROGATOR

That would be my professional recommendation, yes.

> KURT is *thrown* into chair by INTERROGATOR.

GESTAPO INTERROGATOR (cont'd)

We have searched your office and domicile. We found one thousand envelopes addressed to civic leaders throughout the country.

KURT

Christmas cards, merely Christmas cards!

GESTOPO INTERROGATOR

Filled with pamphlets and information praising the illegal Confessional Church, praise for enemies of the fatherland!

KURT

"Joy to the world—"

GESTOPO INTERROGATOR

And another *seven thousand envelopes* yet to be stuffed with such gospel filth!

> GESTOPO INTERROGATOR exits.
> LIGHT only on KURT, who remains sitting in chair.

SK

After six weeks party member Gerstein is released, but—

> KURT stands, starts to exit scene, startled by accusing VOICES.
> VARIOUS VOICES from the shadows UPSTAGE bark out each portion of his freedom's conditions:

VOICE 1

Expelled from the party!

VOICE 2

Dismissed from the Ministry of Mines—

VOICE 3

Barred from public service—

VOICE 1

Forbidden to seek professional employment in the private sector—

VOICE 3

Banned from public speaking anywhere in the Reich!

>THE VOICES depart. KURT is alone on STAGE.

KURT

But if I am to continue my self-imposed task of opposition—

>REGINA enters.

REGINA

Self-imposed? What do you mean? I don't know what you mean; you don't know what you mean. You are pressing too hard on things that will not move, Kurt Erich Gerstein!

KURT

Mountains move!

REGINA

No, mountains are climbed, mountains are conquered, but mountains remain.

KURT

I have been told that mountains move!

REGINA

>(Panicked)

Who told you that?

KURT

And if I am to continue my self-imposed opposition, I must gain readmission to the Party!

REGINA

... pushing against things that will not move.

KURT

It is an absolute prerequisite, without which any freedom of action is nullified!

REGINA

And at what price?

KURT

The *only* price by which reentry into enemy territory may be bought.

REGINA

And what is that?

KURT

By lying! Lying! Lying!

REGINA

(Sobbing)
Who have you become, Kurt Erich Gerstein? Who have you become?!

SK

God's spy is who he has become!

KURT

I am God's spy! Called of the Almighty to sabotage devilish intentions!
FRITZ GERSTEIN, KURT's brother, approaches from behind...

FRITZ

You must petition the Party and beg your reinstatement. The charges and imprisonment have unjustly sullied your character and shamed our family.

KURT

My dear brother, Fritz, come to mend the fence?

FRITZ

I've come to help restore you to a meaningful life.

KURT

It hasn't been meaningful to father, I know. He would have me a quiet engineer praising the wisdom of his order. I'm sure it was his idea to send you.

FRITZ

We would have you reconciled to the Party.

KURT

I will be.

FRITZ

But not on your terms.

    (A beat)

Let me write the reconciling letter for reinstatement to the Party.

KURT

Am I incapable?

FRITZ

Father says you are.

KURT

    (Mockingly in jest)

O, that I brought the joy to his rigid soul that his other sons, his more dutifully ordered sons brought him.

FRITZ

Father says you are incapable.

    A beat.

KURT

Then please write the letter. It will be one less humiliation and, besides, you always had a flair for the overwrought. Beg well; boast

KURT (cont'd)
hard. I will be eternally grateful, or at least until the Third Reich reaches its evolutionary end a thousand years from now.

    FRITZ pulls a letter from HIS pocket, begins reading—

FRITZ
January 1937, Supreme Party Court, Munich: I am bound to resist the charge of having been lacking in fidelity to the National Socialist movement, and of joining those who seek to sabotage the work of the Führer. I am deeply linked with the movement, and it is my most ardent desire to serve it, and to further the work of Adolf Hitler, with all my strength and by all the means in my power, even at the cost of my life. I may have made mistakes, but I cannot feel that they warrant the extreme penalty of my expulsion from the Party. Like any good German, I see in this a slur upon my character which I have not deserved. Most respectfully, Kurt Gerstein.

    LIGHT OUT ON FRITZ. UP ON ELFRIEDE, dressed in modest wedding gown,

REGINA
Later in 1937, he would marry his dear Elfriede.

ELFRIEDE
We met during Christmas of 1930. I was the daughter of a newly installed Protestant minister in Cologne. My brother had made Kurt's acquaintance at the YMCA. I had a friend who invited my brother and me to a Christmas party. I remember it was a long table lighted with candles. Suddenly a door behind me opened, and feeling a draught, I turned around.

KURT
    (Entering, with flowers he gives to ELFRIEDE)
What maniac had the wind blown in?

    KURT pulls up HIS trouser leg to show a portion of HIS bare calf and then strikes a "beauty pose."

KURT (cont'd)
>(Self-mockingly)

All-German male beauty contest, third prize!

ELFRIEDE

I'd never seen another man like him—

KURT

Our eyes immediately met.

ELFRIEDE

Our eyes did meet—

KURT

I was staring. Look at her—she's beautiful!

ELFRIEDE

In a letter he asked me if I smoked. If I did, I would have to give it up.

KURT

I never did see the glamour in cigarettes.

ELFRIEDE

My mother dutifully told me I'd found myself a madman, on the lines of Bismarck!

KURT

With apologies to Herr Bismarck!

ELFRIEDE
>(Smiling)

Yes.

KURT

But joy of joys, Elfriede said "yes."

ELFRIEDE

Yes.

KURT

The loveliness that poured forth and touched this monstrosity!

ELFRIEDE

Yes, I will. And you will let me into those distant rooms of thought that always demand your attention.

KURT

Distant rooms?

ELFRIEDE

I always wonder where you are. In what room are you lounging or angered or sorting?

KURT

We've been over this a few times.

ELFRIEDE

I would only hope that we graciously demand each other's attention.

>ELFRIEDE exits, leaving KURT alone.

KURT

Forgive my eccentricities.

SK

"Months later Gerstein was arrested by order of the Berlin Gestapo, charged with seven other men with plotting to commit high treason. This time he could truthfully deny the charge. He was innocent in fact, if not in feeling."

>KURT curled up on a chair in a darkened portion of the STAGE.

KURT

A mock conspiracy in which I had played no active part. Fools. And for this I sit in despair in a cell I do not deserve. But what do I deserve? A medal for being a good boy? Do I deserve Elfriede, who is rewarded for her fanciful flight into a marital bazaar with the

KURT (cont'd)

slap of an incarcerated husband? I fall indefinitely into the hands of my enemies so soon after hearing the call of God to lift His banner amidst the monstrosities of justice. I cannot sing like an imprisoned Saint Paul. I do not know the passion of Jeremiah.

SK

A leap without an abyss?

KURT

It seems I leap only into walls.

SK

And your leap with Elfriede?

KURT

She sits alone wondering what hand she's been dealt.

SK

And she plays the hand with faithfulness amidst the despair.

KURT

All I know now is she's alone. And I'm alone with the predators that are my solitary thoughts.

    ELFRIEDE enters, never noticing SK.

ELFRIEDE

I miss you, darling Kurt. The morning communion, afternoon embrace, evening prayers, nighttime touch. I miss you, Kurt.

KURT

I am so sorry that you must go through this. Your father must hate me.

ELFRIEDE

He does not hate you.

KURT

Then your mother hates me.

ELFRIEDE
She warned me—

KURT
That I was a madman on the order of

KURT/ELFRIEDE
Bismarck.
    A PAUSE.

ELFRIEDE
Have they told you how long you will be detained?

KURT
That is part of the torture. The short answer is indefinitely.

ELFRIEDE
I'd prefer a long answer.

KURT
    (Panicking)
My dearest, I fear I may never get out. I'm ashamed to say to you that I no longer know what hope feels like. You should never have married me; they will never let me—

ELFRIEDE
Kurt, you must not speak like this! They will let you out.

KURT
How do you know? How do you know?

ELFRIEDE
I just know, dear Kurt.

KURT
I would give five years of my life to hold you right now—

ELFRIEDE

Trust in our God, who assures us through Saint Paul that no temptation has befallen us—

KURT

What is tempting is to stop the fight within my soul. We should not have married! Look what I bring to your table! Not even crumbs!

ELFRIEDE

No, we will survive this. We will talk again at our kitchen table and wonder why we grow old so fast. Do not despair.

KURT

Ten years! Ten years I would give to hold you right now!

>ELFRIEDE starts to walk backward, slowly toward HER exit.

ELFRIEDE

Do not despair, my dear.

KURT

Elfriede, wait. I almost forgot to tell you. Look Elfriede, engraved in the metal of my chair:

>ELFRIEDE stops. KURT goes to chair and reads.

KURT (cont'd)

"Pray, Mother of God will help you." "Pray, Mother of God will help you." It is a comfort to me. My cell has appeared to me as a small church.

>KURT picks up chair and brings it as close as HIS cell allows HIM.

KURT (cont'd)

>(Most passionately)

"I salute with gratitude this unknown brother who sent me this encouragement in my deep affliction. God bless him."

ELFRIEDE

Yes, Kurt.

> KURT, never taking HIS eyes off of ELFRIEDE, puts the chair down.

KURT

And I salute the love of my life, who brings me comfort from God. I love you, my dearest!

> ELFRIEDE exits.
>
> After a PAUSE, SK reappears. KURT is again forlorn.

SK

In the dark you still find yourself chosen.

KURT

Wasting away in this dung heap.

SK

And what of your prison interrogator, Ernst Zerrer?

KURT

What of him?

SK

How is it that an interrogator suddenly changes his tone to one of advocacy?

KURT

He told me he read one of the moral discourses I wrote to urge the youth to purity. He was moved to deliver it to his young son.

SK

And?

KURT

I suddenly appeared to him to no longer be public enemy number one.

KURT (cont'd)
   (Sarcastically)
It was a miracle.

SK

And what of Zerrer letting you fill out the interrogation form? Letting you, the *prisoner*, dictate the contents of your form to *his* secretary?

KURT

What is your point?

SK

You have the ability to engender trust, a trust that opens many gates.

KURT

I'd rather have the gift of juggling.

SK

After your interrogation at Stuttgart, you were sent to the prison at Welzheim—

KURT
   (Still on the juggling theme)
To be able to keep darts and footballs and hard candy in the air—

SK

Why did you get out of the Welzheim prison camp so soon? You were conversing with prison guards, everyone acting like they were old friends.

KURT
   (Coming out of dark mood)
How I have always loved the simple German mind and heart—

SK

Six weeks.

KURT

"I quoted Mark Antony's speech in Julius Caesar, 'Friends, Romans . . .' and used it to illustrate the tricks and subtleties of this world. By the time we got to Welzheim the guards were all on my side."

SK

And for those six weeks you saw others suffering more than you.

KURT

Who knew it would only be six weeks?

SK

Was it Zerrer's influence, a Shakespearean sonnet?

KURT

I saw the vermin, the hunger and cold, the brutality of guards towards prisoners who had no Shakespearean references, and dogs that bit even jugglers.

SK

And others hung themselves, or went mad, or went over to their captors and volunteered to beat their fellow prisoners to save their own skin.

KURT

They made me swear that once released I would divulge nothing of what I had heard or seen to anyone.

SK

You would learn to juggle it all in your mind—

KURT

And keep it from my dear Elfriede.

SK

How can one sing "A Mighty Fortress is Our God" and live with those images?

KURT

Luther sang while thousands of German peasants were crushed.

SK

(Quoting from Luther's hymn)
... And devils. ... We tremble not for him. One little word shall fell him.

KURT

Now I am free to be unemployed, reenter into a familiar melancholy, and offer my wife constant strain, haunted by the threat of Gestapo knocking down our door.

SK

In sickness and in health—

KURT

In madness and mania!

REGINA

You would write a letter to your Uncle Robert in Saint Louis, Missouri, expressing dismay at the Party's attack against the Church, both Catholic and Protestant. You complain that in the minds of the Nazis, the "height of perfection for the boys and girls of Germany is held to be that night and day they should think of no one else but Adolf Hitler and of nothing but Germany." You told him you grievously fear that "a people, and a younger generation, without God were a source of danger."

KURT

Of course. The situation had become terribly serious for me. When Uncle Robert visited Germany, he only saw the Führer's impressive new bridges, paved roads, and efficient train schedules.

SK

You wrote that the question before Germany involved whether she was "to believe that justice is a transcendent concept over which

SK (cont'd)

the human will has no power . . . and that he who talks of justice does so in the name of an all-powerful Supreme Judge to whom he is responsible? Or are we to concede that "the law is whatever serves the people"—that is to say, a purely utilitarian affair?

KURT

"Is Justice to be the harlot of the State?"

SK

And in the next breath you wrote another letter seeking re-admission to the Party, not only proclaiming your Nazi faith, but repudiating Reverend Martin Niemöller, head of the condemned Confessing Church.

KURT

I warned Niemöller more than once "that the leadership he was giving did not suit our young people, who were ardent supporters of the Führer and National Socialism."

REGINA

Which are we to *believe*, Kurt Erich?

KURT

"I wanted back into the Party. My letters were "tactics:" an invitation to misunderstand me." I will learn to *thank* them and move on with my venture.

SK

Sometimes we get what we ask for.

REGINA

The Supreme Tribunal of the Party grants you provisional membership—

KURT

Excluded from State service—

SK

But free to serve in the private sector—

KURT

In a potash mine, the Nazi state desperate for engineers.

(HE poses as for a picture)
Kurt Gerstein, potash mining engineer, duly repentant, last chosen.

REGINA

(Getting up)
But what were you really to do?

KURT

Devote myself to Nazi gatherings, pour myself into the Hitler Youth.

SK

But what were you really to do?

KURT

Unswervingly serve the Führer!

REGINA

Doing what?

KURT

Join the army—I cannot stand on a sideline while my countrymen fight.

SK

No more protesting?

KURT

I am spied on constantly, not free of my past. The waters around me must settle, I am a father now—my infant son must know a man of highest repute. I no longer have time or patience for Niemöller and his Confessional Church. My church will be the Luftwaffe parachute corps.

SK

Is this how the waters settle? Is this how a spy for God escapes being spied upon, by running to someone else's war? Is it your blood shed on the Führer's battlefield that redeems you from disrepute?

KURT

I don't know what redemption is anymore! I only want to be led beside still waters! I am tired of the oppression!

REGINA

And your Good Shepherd doesn't know this?

KURT

Germany has no Good Shepherd; it's every man for himself! I have only one vision now: for my little boy, my wife, and victory for my Führer.

REGINA

But you shall know the truth and the truth will set you free!

SK

Yes, you momentarily allow your ears to be dulled and your eyes closed, but the gift of being trusted endears you to too many at every level of society: industrialists who know the cost of their profits, party leaders shamed by your fits of righteous indignation, political prisoners, potential martyrs, everyone knows more than they care to. And it is your constitution to be more than curious. Yes, you will know the truth. Go ahead, apply for the Luftwaffe; do you think they can use a parachute corp. member who has hurt his foot in a mine accident?

KURT

I am not crippled!

SK

Go ahead, run to the fury of war. Let your conscience be freed by the frenzy of slaughter.

KURT

If I am rejected by the Luftwaffe, I understand there is room in the Waffen SS! Their letter of acceptance or rejection will arrive in the mail soon.

SK

No such letter from God, aye?

REGINA

There is one coming. Your bishop will tell you—

KARL

(Entering)

Kurt, my wife's sister, Berta, has died of cerebral thrombosis. She had been transferred to the clinic in accordance with measures adopted by the Commissioner at the Ministry of Defense. We are told that her severe mental affliction caused her great suffering, and, therefore, we found it easy to accept her death as a merciful release.

KURT

And where is the body?

KARL

We were informed that an epidemic broke out in the clinic, which resulted in the local police ordering the immediate cremation of all corpses—

KURT

Ashes escape autopsies, don't they, Karl?

KARL

(Indignant)

We have no reason to doubt the official explanation!

KURT

And passively submit to authorities in good, pristine German fashion!

KURT (cont'd)

(HE mockingly gives salute, arm rigidly outstretched and remaining so through next few moments)
Heil Hitler! I'm looking for still waters!

KARL

My sister-in-law is dead, and you offer mockery to the Führer! Father warned me you would respond this way!

KURT

Notice the perfectly erect arm, the exacting angle of the hailing hand! I am a perfect Nazi, Karl! Can't you see! I believe what the party pronounces!

KARL

It's a miracle they let you back in.

KURT

(Arm still up)
How could they deny such perfect posture!

KARL starts to walk away.

KURT (cont'd)

And where was your sister-in-law sent to cure her *disease*?

KARL

Hadamar psychiatric hospital. I suppose you know all about it.

KURT

Don't you realize what they did to Berta?

KARL

Like I told you, she died of cerebral thrombosis.

KURT

Hadamar is a slaughterhouse! All mental patients in Germany are being systematically exterminated!

KARL

Cerebral thrombosis!

KURT

Berta was murdered!

KARL

Cerebral thrombosis!

KURT

(Giving "Seig Heil" salute, perfectly)
Cerebral thrombosis!

KARL turns and exits, abruptly.

From UPSTAGE, the farthest distance possible, REGINA appears.

REGINA

Will that be sufficient as a letter from God?

KURT

The mentally ill mercifully relieved of the burden they are to the Fatherland.

REGINA

It's as if Berta hand-delivered the note from heaven itself.

KURT

Germany must not win this war!

SK appears UPSTAGE.

SK

So what are you to *do*?

KURT

There are no still waters. I will seek admission into the Waffen SS. I will not be swayed. I will live in the valley of the shadow of death.

KURT (cont'd)

I will fear evil. God may not be with me. But I intend to find out what's going on.

SK

It is to enter the camp of the powers of evil.

KURT

"Those people are so vicious that they must not and cannot win the war. They're so evil that they will bring down everyone who opposes them with themselves. The only course is to join them, to find out what their plans are and to modify them whenever possible. A person operating within the movement may be able to sidetrack orders or interpret them in his own way. I want to know who gives the orders and who carries them out: who sends people to the concentration camps, who maltreats them and who kills them. I will know them all. And when the end comes I will be one of those who testifies against them."

SK

You see your way clearly then?

KURT

Clearly to hell.

SK

Then to hell you must go! To enter the camp of the powers of evil by faith.

KURT

My promised land is "only one thing: to see to the bottom of this witch-pot and then tell the people what I would have seen there— Even if my life is then threatened." There is no going back. "I have been myself twice betrayed by Nazi agents who infiltrated the Protestant Church and prayed close to me." I am confident that Nazi infiltrations can be reversed. What they can do, I can do better. As a member of the SS I will plot and secretly sabotage them. They

KURT (cont'd)

have murdered thousands of Bertas, I will witness, report, and murder their plans.

> KURT is brought out and handed the SS Stormtrooper uniform by

SLIDE SIX: Sergeant Robert Weigelt, training instructor for Waffen SS.

WEIGELT

> (Handing KURT a shirt)

Try this on. I've concluded that your body wasn't made for any uniform. Nothing, absolutely nothing fits. Hurry and try this hat on . . . I can't wait to see the mockery it makes of your head.

> KURT tries on the hat.

WEIGELT (cont'd)

This is my last attempt. We will stay with it, whatever the—

KURT

I think this one's it—

WEIGELT

Look at it sit awkwardly on that head of yours—

KURT

I can only imagine, sir—

WEIGELT

> (Looking him over)

Your belt sags, this uniform hangs in folds. You are far from the ideal soldier, Gerstein.

KURT

I can only imagine, sir—

WEIGELT

(In KURT's face, now the drill sergeant)
Possibly the exact opposite of the ideal soldier.

    KURT is working hard at getting HIS uniform to fit.

WEIGELT (cont'd)

All this might be manageable if you could but march properly. It is impossible for you to find the slightest rhythm, and your zealous attempts are only throwing everyone else off!

KURT

I am an incurable klutz!

    WEIGELT starts clapping his hands to mark the beat and SINGS aloud a German anthem.

WEIGELT

Try it again; I'm waiting for a miracle! March, Stormtrooper Kurt Gerstein! March! You must keep step or you will fail your training! Follow me!

    WEIGELT begins to goosestep, still clapping his hands, singing the anthem. KURT attempts but is pitifully inept.
    WEIGELT stops, KURT stops.

WEIGELT (cont'd)

Keep going!

    KURT does. WEIGELT continues to clap hands and sing, though softer through narration below.

SK

Such marching incompetence should have been reported to the SS authorities. Sergeant Weigelt, for whatever reason, could not, would not bring himself to do it. He had become another captive of Kurt Gerstein. On the day his training group was inspected for marching precision, Sergeant Weigelt arranged for Gerstein to visit the sickbay. His inability to goosestep was never discovered.

REGINA

Nor was Kurt's brief absence without leave ever reported by Weigelt. His group had been transferred to Holland by train. Upon departing the train, Weigelt noted one missing soldier. After marching the rest to the barracks, the sergeant waited by the guardhouse, only to find his wayward Stormtrooper show up riding a bicycle. At the momentary confusion at the train station, Kurt had slipped off to visit friends.

>KURT and WEIGELT are now on opposite sides of the STAGE. WEIGELT comes storming up to KURT.

WEIGELT

Where have you been?!

KURT

Don't bawl me out here. I've bought you some Schnapps and cigarettes. Let's go inside.

>KURT exits. WEIGELT is speechless, stunned by KURT's audacity, HE can only watch KURT walk away. After a beat, WEIGELT follows.

SK

This was the start of the conspiratorial relationship between Gerstein and Weigelt . . .

SLIDE SEVEN: Spring 1941. Kurt Gerstein assigned to the Waffen SS Ministry of Hygiene in Berlin. His duties come under the general heading, "Decontamination."

SLIDE EIGHT: He was tattooed with the letters AB, blood-group IV. His SS number 417,460.

SLIDE NINE: Ernst Weisenfeld, former member of the Protestant Youth

ERNST

"We arranged to meet in Berlin, near the Tiergarten. He arrived on the dot, as I had been sure he would, and at the sight of him I

ERNST (cont'd)

burst out laughing. So did he. It was that SS uniform!" I remember him saying:

KURT

You know, there are some extraordinary characters in the SS—

ERNST

"By which he meant diabolical characters that needed to be carefully studied and also misguided idealists whose attitude to life was totally different from his own. It horrified him to find men whom he detested in charge of the machine, possessors of such immense power and exercising it with such cold-blooded passion"—

KURT

But it is all so fascinating!

ERNST

"It was his unbounding, insatiable curiosity, a passionate desire to know. If he was Christian in his love of his fellow-men, he was at the same time Faust the experimenter."

SK

He joined the SS at exactly the right time, becoming quickly trusted by the head of Ministry of Hygiene. His ascendancy was procured by a typhoid outbreak on the Russian front in '41. By the end of the year ten thousand had been infected in the German army. The outbreak became a top priority of the Reich and fell under the jurisdiction of the Ministry of Hygiene. The Ministry Chief, Joachim Mrugowsky, was at his wits end, and anyone who could provide a solution would win his undying gratitude.

REGINA

Enter Kurt Gerstein.

> KURT crosses to DOWN CENTER, with great enthusiasm pitches his solution.

KURT

It is not that difficult, really: obviously a problem of decontamination, basically of water supplies, uniforms, cooking utensils—basically everything! First, we'll draw up a delousing apparatus for everything, using high pressure steam—it will destroy all contaminants, not only the lice but also their excrement, and secondly, a mobile water-filter unit.

WEIGELT

Gerstein's proposals are approved enthusiastically by the army and mass produced at factories in Munich and Celle and rushed to the Russian front. The Chief, Mrugowsky, is ecstatic . . . comes to regard him as a "positive genius of sanitation." He skips all non-commissioned grades!

KURT
    (To WEIGELT)
And believe it or not, Robert, the Chief instructed his secretary never to question any of my requirements!

WEIGELT
What?!

KURT
Special authorizations, safe-conducts, reserved train compartments, official cars—

WEIGELT
Kurt Gerstein?!

KURT
I was to have anything I asked for—ordered by the Chief of the Department of Sanitation!

WEIGELT
The Reich is upside down!

KURT

    (Laughing)
Robert, dear friend, I have become the blue-eyed boy in SS sanitation!

WEIGELT

You believe you can derail the Reich?

KURT

It is a train headed for hell, of course. And I am assigned as a conductor.

WEIGELT

You believe this nonsense despite all evidence to the contrary!

KURT

And first, I will conquer the Ministry by surrounding myself with old and trusted friends, arranging transfers from various fronts—

WEIGELT

Rising in the ranks, day after day—

KURT

    (Performs perfect salute)
"Heil Hitlers."

WEIGELT

Despite carrying a clothes brush in your revolver holster.

KURT

The hardware's too heavy!

WEIGELT

Your service pistol in a drawer of your desk.

KURT

You don't need a gun on shopping trips.

WEIGELT

And somehow, you're retrieving lists of concentration camps

WEIGELT (cont'd)

residents, and proceeding to leave them readily available on your desk—sending a hand-printed invitation to be caught because you miss being a prisoner of the Reich!

KURT

Aren't we all prisoners of the Reich?

WEIGELT

Everyone in the department seems to "like" your constant array of presents, as though every other week was Christmas.

KURT

Life would be better if every other week was Christmas!

WEIGELT

It would be better if I didn't trust you, Kurt Gerstein.

KURT

Would it be better if Mrugowsky didn't trust me?
  (HE laughs)
How is one to explain that I am the head of the SS Ministry of Hygiene?

WEIGELT

He is indebted.

KURT

My department is concerned with everything involving decontamination and disinfection—

WEIGELT

Including the use of gas.

KURT

  (Posing)
The great white chief of water purification!

WEIGELT

One day we were having a drink at the Ministry . . .

> KURT and WEIGELT move to small table and two chairs DOWNSTAGE, they sit.

WEIGELT (cont'd)

A man enters, I presumed a doctor—

> A DOCTOR enters.

DOCTOR

> (To KURT)

We need two trucks capable of pumping exhaust gas into a closed chamber.

KURT

What?

DOCTOR

Two trucks for pumping exhaust gas into a closed area.

KURT

Why?

DOCTOR

Party necessity.

KURT

Why diesel exhaust into a closed area?

DOCTOR

We are at war, sir. It is enough to know the machinery of war requires lubrication. I am told you are a specialist in handling dangerous gases.

WEIGELT

Kurt Gerstein is the golden boy of Waffen SS, Ministry of Hygiene—

DOCTOR

Solve our problem; that is an order!

    A PAUSE.

KURT

That is not hard to figure out. Let me show you . . .

    (HE begins to draw a design on paper)
"You need only fit the trucks with an auxiliary engine."

DOCTOR

What kind?

KURT

For instance, a Sachs Diesel would do excellently for pumping out exhaust gas.

    CROSSFADE . . .

SK

No one knows if Gerstein ever heard from the doctor again. Since the beginning of the Russian campaign a secret group of specialists had been trying to find a way of liquidating large populations without the use of machine guns—

REGINA

Too demoralizing for execution squads—

SK

And too noisy. In White Russia, the method of pumping exhaust gases from a vehicle into a closed chamber had been tried and found wanting. The victims had to be finished off with bombs, under the watchful eyes of the experimenters.

REGINA

Later, a method of mass extermination involved a truck with a sealed back was packed with people. The exhaust gases being funneled through a pipe. The frantic victims pushed to the back of the truck, tipping it up.

SK

"Modifications were called for." And, if we are to believe his witnesses, Kurt Gerstein was unwittingly drawn into the dark center of such modifications.

KURT

>   (An agonized cry)
> What have I done?

SLIDE TEN: Spring, 1942, Gerstein visits his friend Helmut Franz, recovering from wounds.
>   KURT crosses DOWNSTAGE to bedside of HELMUT.

KURT

>   (Constantly glancing over his shoulder, fearing someone catching him in his self-exposure, loud whisper)
> What is the secret? I went to Tiergarten Synagogue where Jews of all ages were kept under police guard for a night and a day. I am an SS officer wearing my SS uniform—and I ask
>   (Assumes "SS voice")
> Why are these people here and where are they being taken? And none of those police bastards would say a word. The next night they are all gone, whisked away to an unknown destination. What is the secret?

HELMUT

It is not for you to know the secret. It is kept safely by our Führer, for whom I am gladly wounded.

KURT

For whom are these Jews "gladly wounded?" You are a fool! You trust Herr Hitler with this secret?!

HELMUT

I have no secret and I don't want to know what I shouldn't. I only want to heal of my wounds in the quickest way possible.

KURT

In my quest of the secret, I went to the institute in Riga, hearing that many Jewish girls had been sent there.

HELMUT

For what?

KURT

I know for a fact that human specimens have been required there on which to feed typhus-infected fleas and all I find are frightened girls filling the institute—all unable, unwilling to tell me anything!

HELMUT

You are the fool! Who would expect them to say anything to a stranger in an SS uniform? You know more then you let on, Kurt Gerstein. You know more than those girls, don't you?

KURT

I know that the concentration camps have as their nerve center the SS Office of Economy and Administration, and that the Ministry of Hygiene is financed from this source.
    (Leaning into HELMUT)
And it is there, pushing bribes wholesale that I shall go searching for informants and allies.

HELMUT

Informants and allies for what?

KURT

I think I have accidentally aided in the extermination of Jews.
    A PAUSE.

HELMUT

Why do you tell me such things?

KURT

There is no one else to tell.

HELMUT

Tell your wife.

KURT

She must know nothing of my espionage.

HELMUT

Espionage? I thought you were telling me of accidentally murdering God's chosen people.

KURT

If I breathe a word of any of this to Elfriede and then choose to flee from my SS post, the party will torture her for information and then kill her, along with every other person who vouched for my character upon entering into SS officer training.

HELMUT

If you fled, "God would condemn you as a deserter."

KURT

And I would deserve condemnation.

HELMUT

If it is Jews you care about, then do something.

KURT

What? Blow myself up?! Tell my colleagues that the Jews must be evacuated at once?! Then they will say, "Fine, go right ahead, make the arrangements with Churchill, Stalin, and Roosevelt." And I will only be reminded of my powerlessness.

    A NURSE enters to check on HELMUT.

NURSE

Is everything okay in here?

HELMUT

Fine. Fine. I am visited by my old friend. He used to be a father to hundreds of us before the war.

The NURSE exits.

HELMUT (cont'd)
(Grabs KURT by lapel, pulls HIM closer to his face)
You are no longer the same Kurt Gerstein I knew, are you?

KURT
No.

HELMUT
I used to call you "Vati." You *were* a father to me. But now you frighten all hope of a future worth healing for. I suppose you want me orphaned of these things.

KURT
I only want you to keep my secrets and assist me in finding others.

HELMUT
I have enough secrets of my own.

KURT
You don't think God knows your secrets?

HELMUT
You don't think God knows Nazi secrets?

SLIDE ELEVEN: Major Rolf Günther, Central Security Office, Günther's boss was Adolf Eichmann . . .

GÜNTHER enters to another part of the STAGE

GÜNTHER
"Lieutenant Gerstein—

KURT is startled, looks up and finds GÜNTHER, carrying a BRIEFCASE.

GÜNTHER (cont'd)
Lieutenant Kurt Gerstein, you are required to procure 260 kilos of prussic acid within the shortest possible time."

KURT crosses to GÜNTHER.

KURT

For what purpose?

GÜNTHER

Purpose?! Sufficient to know, Lieutenant Gerstein, that our Führer is the potter, we are the clay. You will be informed of the "method of transport and where the prussic acid is to be delivered. You are also assigned to accompany it and to arrange for its application in place of the gas now being used."

KURT

Top secret?

GÜNTHER

(Starts to exit)
It must be, if possible, a secret kept from the gods.
>GÜNTHER hands KURT the briefcase.
>GÜNTHER proceeds to exit.

KURT

(Calling to GÜNTHER)
So, therefore, excluded from any prayer?

GÜNTHER

You are the clay, Lieutenant Gerstein, just the clay.
>GÜNTHER exits.

HELMUT

(Calling from dimly lit hospital bed)
Vati! Vati! You don't think God knows Nazi secrets?

KURT

He surely knows my secrets.

HELMUT

So you are the clay.

>   KURT crosses to HELMUT.

KURT

>   (Agitated)

I also know God has secrets of his own.

HELMUT

And you press to pry them loose?

>   KURT opens the briefcase, pulls out the SS letter, bordered in red, and shows it to HELMUT.

KURT

Do you see this?

HELMUT

I am not blind!

KURT

"This consignment is intended to kill thousands of people—you know what I mean, the sort of people who are labeled sub-human."

HELMUT

>   (Hands over ears)

I do not want to hear your secrets!

KURT

>   (Pulling at HELMUT's arms)

Helmut, what am I supposed to do? If I carry out this order I shall be an accomplice in mass extermination!

HELMUT

I don't know! Leave me alone!

KURT

>(Increase panic)

It is you that I can talk to! The thought of suicide is constantly before me.

HELMUT

Do not tell me these things, Kurt Gerstein; I beg you!

KURT

"I want to commit suicide, but if I do two other men will die. Every member of the SS is vouched for by two others. If I kill myself, they'll both be shot!" And what of Elfriede and my children?! What will become of them?

HELMUT

I don't—

KURT

You know the Bible, what does it tell me?!

HELMUT

Let go—

KURT

>(Screams)

Thou shalt not kill!

>The NURSE enters.

NURSE

There is only agitation every time you visit my patient.

>KURT quickly finds his composure.

HELMUT

My friend is only telling me the highlights of Sunday's sermon.

NURSE

I'm glad I didn't hear it.

HELMUT

The sermon moved few.

NURSE

Sir, you must leave at once.

> KURT puts the SS letter back in the briefcase, and begins to exit.

HELMUT

Vati!

> KURT stops.

HELMUT (cont'd)

Only two will be shot.

> KURT exits.

END OF ACT ONE

Act Two

> In another portion of the STAGE, canisters (boxes) piled up, depicting prussic acid being transported. KURT crosses to them.

KURT
Stop the transport!
> A driver, German SOLDIER, enters from behind the boxes . . .

SOLDIER
But, why, Lieutenant Gerstein?

KURT
What is that I smell?

SOLDIER
I don't smell anything.
> KURT sniffs around the cargo.

KURT
It's leaking. The acid is leaking.
> SOLDIER starts to sniff around.

SOLDIER
I don't smell—

KURT
You have not been trained to smell the faintest of smells.
> KURT goes to one of the boxes, inhales.

KURT (cont'd)

It's this one.

SOLDIER

What?

KURT

This one is leaking. We'll have to ditch the whole load at once—

SOLDIER

What?!

KURT

The whole load! It's a matter of life and death!

SOLDIER

But—

KURT

At once!

SOLDIER

But we'll have to return to the factory and start all over!

KURT

Would you rather die in an explosion?! We must get rid of this load and return to Germany for a fresh shipment.

>KURT and the SOLDIER begin to remove the boxes OFFSTAGE.
>THEY continue to unload during the narrative below.

SK

Gerstein quickly assessed that no one knew the game he was playing. He could declare any consignment defective and order its immediate destruction.

REGINA

His word would be enough.

SK

He knew the factories produced decontaminating poisons in doses beyond that required for lice and rodents. Kurt Gerstein was but a child's finger in a dike, moments from bursting forth with destructive fury.

SLIDE TWELVE: Belzec Concentration Camp, Poland

SK (cont'd)

His shipments of prussic acid would inevitably reach their intended destination.

REGINA

His orders were to observe the prussic acid's effectiveness.

    KURT crosses to a doorway frame.

SK

His eyes, his ears, his nostrils were filled with the horrors his hands would later record.

    EXTRAS (the number depends upon availability of production) clustered in terror, move to the barks and whips of GUARDS.

    KURT writing in journal. In disbelief, he tries desperately to maintain some kind of emotional control.

KURT

"Then the march began. Barbed wire on both sides and two dozen Ukrainians behind them, armed with rifles. . . . I stood outside the death chamber with the (camp commander) and some of the police. They were all stark naked, men, women, girls, children, babes in arms, and people with only one leg, all naked. . . ."

GUARD 1

"Don't worry, you aren't going to be hurt. Take deep breaths; it strengthens the lungs—a precaution against disease."

GUARD 2

"The men will have to work, building roads and houses. The women will do the housework and the cooking."

REGINA

"As though the smell were not in their nostrils," and the masses of flies not buzzing around them!

SK

And they must hurry, must not linger "in this threshold to the gates of Hell!"

REGINA

Moving up the stairs, forced beyond their freezing fears—

SK

They saw the "open doors of the chambers on either side of the corridor."

KURT

(With journal)

And then, from those throats "dried with thirst and terror," there arose the notes of the Kaddish—

REGINA

The prayer for all men—

KURT

Believers and unbelievers alike—

SK

The immemorial prayer for orphans—

REGINA

"The song of praise and thanksgiving rising from a submissive earth to an eternally victorious Heaven."

> Perhaps behind scrim, speaking the Kaddish OR done in BLACKOUT with VOICEOVERS. Each VICTIM repeats their prayers/chants throughout scene.

VICTIM 1
Extolled and hallowed be the name of God throughout the world which He has created according to His will. And may He speedily establish His Kingdom of righteousness on earth.

VICTIM 2
Amen.

VICTIM 3
Praised be His glorious name unto all eternity.

VICTIM 4
Praised and glorified be the name of the Holy One, though He be above all the praises which we can utter. Our guide is He in life and our redeemer through all eternity.

VICTIM 1
Our help cometh from Him, the creator of heaven and earth.

VICTIM 4
The departed whom we now remember have entered into the peace of life eternal. They still live on earth in the acts of goodness they performed and in the hearts of those who cherish their memory. May the beauty of their life abide among us as a loving benediction.

VICTIM 2
And may the Father of peace send peace to all who mourn, and comfort all the bereaved among us.
> LIGHTS UP.
> WIRTH, a Nazi commander of the camp, enters.

WIRTH
Stuff them in tight!
> VICTIMS shoved through the threshold and doorframe with KURT nearby.
> VICTIMS praying/chanting continues.
> The CACAPHONY INCREASES IN VOLUME.

WIRTH (cont'd)

(Shouting)

Seven to eight hundred to each chamber! Make it happen!

KURT

(Shouting)

Seven to eight hundred human beings in an area of 270 square feet? It isn't possible!

WIRTH

It is possible!

KURT

It is impossible to—

WIRTH

Many are children, many more are very small. It can be done! It must be done!

A GUARD RUSHES IN.

GUARD

(To WIRTH)

The diesel engine has stalled—

WIRTH

Get it started! I don't care what it takes! The fumes must fill the chambers! I will not tolerate malfunction!

GUARD

We are trying as best we can!

KURT

For two hours and forty-nine minutes by my watch!

REGINA

Then, finally, the engine was fixed.

SK

The lights in the chamber went on and guests were invited to watch through peepholes while the exhaust fumes took hold of their victims.

> The cacophony of prayers, chants, build to a crescendo for 32 seconds.

KURT

Thirty-two minutes later it was over. The Diesel was switched off and the discharge doors opened. I looked inside the open doors of the chamber and saw the upright bodies packed inside, "awaiting the right to fall down." All of the dead, "like marble statue, stood closely one to another . . . Members of one family could be easily recognized; clutched to each other by their stiffened hands. It was difficult to separate them."

SK

"Bodies with their arms round each other were sent rolling in the dust of the yard at the far end of the shed. Children's bodies were tossed through the air."

WIRTH

Hurry up! We are behind schedule!

KURT

"The entrance doors opened and the next consignment flowed in up the steps as though on a conveyor-belt."

REGINA

"In the yard, workers searched the bodies for valuables—"

> WIRTH approaches KURT, holding a medal box. HE opens it, shows contents to KURT.

WIRTH

Have a look at this, Lieutenant. "Nothing but gold teeth, and only two days' bag—yesterday and the day before."

SLIDE THIRTEEN: Pastor Kurt Rehling

REHLING

He came to visit me in a state of terrible agitation.

> KURT crosses to REHLING.

KURT

And they kept screaming, "Help us! Help us!" And I was only a witness to the efficiency of my diesel engine methods!

REHLING

And no one does anything, except wonder whether it is better to be killed in the light or in the dark?

KURT

> (Snapping to)

"You must realize that all this is a State secret. Anyone who divulges it, and anyone who listens, is risking death. You and I are now both in danger of our lives."

REHLING

"We ought to shout the truth from the steps of the Town Hall. I must proclaim it from the pulpit."

KURT

> (Throwing up HIS hands)

"Not a newspaper would report it. There would simply be a news item the next day saying that a respected Protestant pastor had had to be hurriedly removed to a mental hospital. And there you'd be forced to give me away, and my friends as well, and we wouldn't be able to help anyone."

REHLING

Perhaps we ought to be thinking less of our chances of success and more of our moral duty.

KURT

"There's no sense in being rash and endangering others. This ring I'm wearing contains a poison capsule—cyanide. If I'm caught, I

KURT (cont'd)

shall use it to make sure I don't betray my friends. Under torture a man will say anything."

REHLING

Your suicide escapes the evil?

KURT

Who can trust what they would spill under threat of unimaginable torture?

REHLING

And if on the other side of the Jordan you are welcomed into a lake of fire?

KURT

No one is to know the horrors I have seen!

REHLING

You don't want me to preach about it?

KURT

Not even to your wife!

REHLING

What about your Elfriede?

KURT

She must know nothing.

    A PAUSE.

REHLING

No, Kurt, the only escape is to stand and proclaim!

KURT

No!

REHLING
So what are we to do?!
> A PAUSE. KURT is frantic.
> REHLING notices an automatic pistol in KURT's holster.

REHLING (cont'd)
I see you have now taken to brandishing a pistol in that holster instead of your menacing SS clothes brush.
> A brief PAUSE.

REHLING (cont'd)
So a bullet instead of cyanide?

KURT
Since Belzec I knew there might be need to kill someone.

REHLING
To be absent from the body is to be present with the Lord.

KURT
Tell that to the shaven heads, the naked throngs, the buried faithful.

REHLING
Kurt, if you are still alive, then it is an invitation to *do* something!

KURT
What do you want me to do?!

REHLING
Do something!

KURT
What?!

REHLING
God told you to join the SS?

KURT

Maybe it was an inner impression, maybe a demonic oppression!

REHLING

Was it the same demon that told you to shout down a Nazi play from the comfort of your seat? Was it the devil that commanded you to distribute anti-Nazi leaflets?

KURT
>(Grabbing REHLING, violently)

Was it a devil that got me into the SS? You are a pastor of the flock, a minister to the lost; you tell me what it was!

>A PAUSE. KURT, realizing that he has grabbed REHLING, snaps out of it.

KURT (cont'd)
>(Quietly)

What am I to do?

REHLING

Continue to tell fellow gospel witnesses.

KURT

Who?

REHLING

Leaders of the Confessing church—Niemöller, Bonhoeffer, and the rest.

KURT

They'll be dismissed as anti-German liars and lunatics. There is no hierarchical authority to leverage repentance!

REHLING

Then go to sympathetic shepherds of the Lutheran Church!

KURT

Like I have gone to you? And they preach the horrifying truth from

KURT (cont'd)

their pulpits and are arrested for lies against the State. Or they are dismissed as no longer fit for service to German saints because of their disgruntled spirit. The perpetrators of this annihilation of European Jews stop at nothing to keep this secret.

REHLING

So you are telling me that they compliment the German hoards by assuming that they would rise up in protest and stop the slaughter if they only knew?

KURT

I believe Hitler, Heyrich, Goebbels—they all fear that. And you are right; such fears are a compliment to the German collective conscience.

REHLING

But is it a warranted compliment?

KURT

Only God knows, Pastor Rehling; only God knows.

REHLING

God knows, aye?

    No response from KURT.

REHLING (cont'd)

So in your mind, there is still a God who knows and decides?

    A PAUSE.

KURT

Is it faith to say I hope so?

REHLING

Saint James says it is faith to *do* something, Kurt.

    A PAUSE.

KURT

The Confessing Church is already branded as traitors. The State Church is acquiescent to the charms of their Arian messiah.

REHLING

Not all members—

KURT

You are the lunatic, radical fringe dismissed by the comfortable minds enjoying the tranquility that still dominates Berlin. I must tell the church with the hierarchical leverage and moral authority to stop the carnage.

REHLING

The Roman Catholic?

KURT

Both of us Protestants, yet we know the Roman Catholic Church is our only ecclesiastical hope. In this moment, for the first time in my life, I regret the Reformation.

REHLING

So whom do you tell? The priest across the street?

KURT

I will begin by pounding on the pope's door.

REHLING

In your SS uniform? Won't he be delighted?

KURT

One quarter of the SS are Catholics. He should be used to it by now.

REHLING

They're not pounding on his door.

KURT

They should be.

KURT begins to walk to another portion of the STAGE.

KURT (cont'd)
(To REHLING, over HIS shoulder)
Half the population of Hitler's Greater Reich is Catholic, as is the Führer himself.

REHLING
And their priests are not privy to State salary. Kurt, this is what must be done.

KURT
Luther has failed us.

REHLING
First storm the door of the Berlin Nuncio. The German representative of Pope Pius XII is your path of action. That is the work of faith.

KURT
In the name of Christ I will boldly proclaim all that I have seen and heard.

REHLING
Of course, you will need an appointment. Orsenigo is a very busy man.

KURT
Appointments are unnecessary; requests for an audience are only invitations for rejections from underlings. I will proceed unannounced in faith. We must watch the Red Sea part before us—to save Jews from the wrath of a new Pharaoh.

REHLING
Without an appointment?

KURT
It seems we are all swine. I'll simply provide a hefty bribe for an underling.

SLIDE FOURTEEN: The Berlin Nuncio, Cesare Orsenigo, papal representative in Germany

ORSENIGO
Who are you? And how did you get in without an appointment?

KURT
The hand of God.

ORSENIGO
And does the hand of God get you the best tables at restaurants without an appointment?

KURT
If necessary, his hand will work in the same way.

ORSENIGO
So who are you?

KURT
Lieutenant Kurt Gerstein, Waffen SS Ministry of Hygiene.

ORSENIGO
What can I do for you?

KURT
I have been an eyewitness to the mass murder of tens of thousands of Jews at the Belzec concentration camp in Poland. Every day, many hundreds at a time are crammed naked into chambers where diesel gases flow in and exterminate the naked, sometimes praying, sometimes screaming children of Israel. Men, women, children—

ORSENIGO
(Cutting off)
Stop!

> KURT is stopped in tracks, stunned by the force of ORSENIGO's voice.
> A PAUSE. Then suddenly,

ORSENIGO (cont'd)

Go away! Get out!

> KURT slowly backs away, more stunned, still facing ORSENIGO.

KURT

But you must tell—

ORSENIGO

I've told you, I will hear nothing more!

> A longer PAUSE. They face each other without further movement.

KURT

(To himself)
Is *this* the hand of God? Has the Church forfeited the right to represent Christ on earth?

> CROSSFADE.
> KURT crosses to a table where ELFRIEDE, his wife, is sitting. HE sits across from HER. SHE is pregnant.
> A long PAUSE.

ELFRIEDE

Kurt, darling, tell me. Please give me a word. What is wrong?

> KURT only looks at HER and stares blankly.
> A longer PAUSE.

ELFRIEDE (cont'd)

I am married to a ghost, Kurt Gerstein. You come and you go like the wind, but we, your family, are a ship without sails to you.

> KURT only continues to stare blankly, as in a trance.

ELFRIEDE (cont'd)

Say something to me, darling Kurt. Tell me, please, please, what is wrong.

Still nothing.

ELFRIEDE (cont'd)
Then why do you come home only to torture your family with silence? What is the agony you keep from us?

ELFRIEDE gets up, crosses away from KURT.

ELFRIEDE (cont'd)
I will wake the children who must see their father!

KURT crosses to HER.

KURT
No, Elfriede.

ELFRIEDE takes a step away from KURT, going to wake the children.

ELFRIEDE
I must wake the children.

KURT grabs HER arm.

KURT
No, my darling Elfriede, please. Let them sleep as long as they can.

ELFRIEDE
Let me go, Kurt, I must wake them. Let me go!

SHE breaks away, HE follows.

KURT
No, please!

SHE turns to HIM.

ELFRIEDE
All I want is to see you hold them, see that you love them, that you will live for them!

KURT

(Screams)
I cannot hold them!

    Startled by HIS outburst, SHE stops.
    A PAUSE.

ELFRIEDE

(With back to KURT)
Then I do not believe that you love them. Then I have no faith that you fight to live for them.

    A PAUSE.

ELFRIEDE (cont'd)

Then it would be best to let them sleep.

KURT

It would be better if I died on the front.

ELFRIEDE

Then what of this child?
    (SHE looks at her belly)
So we must be ready for a fatherless world?

KURT

I don't know . . . I don't know, Elfriede.

ELFRIEDE

(Increased exasperation)
For months I am with the children waiting for a word. You come and you go and we know nothing. So I continue to press on. I wash the dishes, scrub the floors and they only get dirty again. I dust and the dust returns. The children cry and I wipe their tears and then they cry again. Adelheid has been ill it seems forever. They want their Papa. I tell them "Maybe today, maybe today." And then tomorrow I say, "Maybe today, maybe today." And then I comfort myself and say, "Maybe today, maybe today." And today has

ELFRIEDE (cont'd)

arrived. Yet you come only to confirm that you are a shadow your family can no longer hold. What demon possesses you, Kurt Gerstein? Frau Gerstein wants to know.

    A PAUSE.

KURT

Frau Gerstein...

    (THEIR eyes meet)

to tell you it is a demon of hopelessness is to tell you more than you should know.

ELFRIEDE

How is the knowledge of your children safe and asleep in their bed a picture of hopelessness? When is your unborn child a sign of this? When is your wife who loves you a sign of this?

KURT

I have seen a legion of demons and Jesus is nowhere.

ELFRIEDE

Tell me of what you have seen! What do you mean Jesus is nowhere?

KURT

It is a horror—

ELFRIEDE

Our Savior is with us even to the ends of the earth—

KURT

I am afraid it is ended for me.

ELFRIEDE

    (Agitated)

What has ended? What do you mean Jesus is nowhere? Without our faith there is nothing, Kurt, nothing! What have you seen that has so disturbed you?

> SHE crosses to HIM, grabs the arms at HIS side and begins to shake HIM.

ELFRIEDE (cont'd)
I beg you to tell me what it is! "No temptation has seized you except what is common to man. And God is faithful; he will not let you be tempted beyond what you can bear." What, Kurt Gerstein, is so terrible that would deny the Word of God?! What?!

> KURT crumbles to the ground in a heap, weeping. ELFRIEDE goes to HER knees, HER hands caressing HIS face.

ELFRIEDE (cont'd)
My darling, my darling what has come over you? Should I call a doctor?

> KURT shakes HIS head, "no."

ELFRIEDE (cont'd)
Is there any comfort, anything? Am I not a comfort to you, Kurt? Is not your home a comfort, your children? Is there no comfort in the presence and sovereignty of God?

> KURT trying to find HIS equilibrium, finally is able to get out—

KURT
There is no comfort, none in the universe. And I have brought you nothing but constant turmoil.

ELFRIEDE
No, Kurt, we are blessed.

KURT
I am ashamed of blessings now.

ELFRIEDE
What are you saying?

KURT

The doors of hope have been shut, Elfriede. There is no light; there is no justice.

>ELFRIEDE gets up, crosses away from KURT.

ELFRIEDE

Kurt, what am I to do? What am I to do? Do you insult your own wife and children by seeing no light or justice here? Then why bother building a home? Kurt, why bother?!

KURT

I am so sorry, my dear. But it seems I have nothing but burden. Forgive me, forgive me.

ELFRIEDE

Forgive you for what? What?—For seeing things that possess you with melancholy? Things that disinterest you in the comfort of your wife and children?

KURT

I am sorry that I brought you into this marriage of pain.

ELFRIEDE

Will you also apologize for undeniable joys?

>BLACKOUT.

SLIDE FIFTEEN: Baron Göran von Otter, Secretary of the Swedish Embassy

OTTER

Kurt and I were seated in the darkened corridor of the train from Warsaw to Berlin. He had valiantly attempted an expressionless face, but could contain himself no longer. He would break into sobs and only state two words, two words I shall never forget—"Something appalling, something appalling." We were sufficiently isolated so as not to create a stirring. Then he unburdened himself and disclosed everything, begging me to inform my superiors in Sweden.

OTTER (cont'd)
Several months later we would arrange for a meeting on a street in Berlin near our embassy.

>OTTER crosses to a waiting KURT.

KURT
You understand that I couldn't call on you openly, or phone or write.

OTTER
Of course.

KURT
Have you been able to do anything?

OTTER
As you requested, and as was necessary, I have informed my superiors of what you have told me.

KURT
And?

OTTER
I don't know if this has had any result.

KURT
What?!

OTTER
Kurt, I am afraid it is unlikely.

KURT
>(Protesting)

Unlikely?

OTTER
Perhaps you have overestimated the power of foreign statesmen in such matters.

KURT

So the fact that nothing is done with the information is tied to a lack of power from people with great power?

OTTER

I am disappointed, too, but I don't know what—(else I can do)

KURT

>(Getting more agitated and louder with each of the following sentences)

So is everyone else disappointed. Hundreds of thousands of Jews murdered by Nazis and everyone is merely disappointed! Where is the Jewish prophet Amos to condemn the Christian Gentiles—we still on our beds engraved with ivory, lounge on our couches, feast on fattened calf, strum on our harps like David, find the time to improvise on our musical instruments. We drink wine by the bowlful, and use the finest of lotions, but don't do *anything* about the demise and destruction of Jews.

OTTER

>(Loud whisper, looking over his shoulder)

Gerstein, you are getting too loud. Do you want to get us in trouble?

KURT

Do you know where the prophet Amos is today?

OTTER

No, settle down.

KURT

Settle down?!

>OTTER starts to walk away. KURT follows HIM.

KURT (cont'd)

Do you know where Amos is?

OTTER

(Turning around, scolding in loud whisper)
No, I have no idea where an obscure prophet of Israel is at this moment.

KURT

He's inhaling diesel exhaust in a Polish wilderness.

>OTTER pulls away, starts to exit. HE then stops and turns to KURT.

OTTER

We did what we could with the information. As far as my country goes, you must leave it at that. And you must be more discreet, no more outbursts or you are asking for trouble.

KURT

We have met on an isolated street. No one has heard anything. Don't worry.

OTTER

So your outbursts are that calculated?

KURT

I have not been caught; I do not wish to be caught.

OTTER

Well, we have done what we can.

>Again, OTTER starts to leave.

KURT

I have heard my name mentioned in a BBC German broadcast—

OTTER

(Loud whisper, scolding)
You are a fool to mention such things in public.

KURT

What things?

OTTER

The BBC—that you listen to them at all. You know the ban on such activities.

KURT

There is absolutely no one here. What are you afraid of—microphones built into these alleys?

OTTER

What more do you want, Lieutenant Gerstein?

KURT

The broadcast named me as one of the Nazi criminals running concentration camps and noted that I was concerned with experiments on human guinea pigs.

OTTER

What?

KURT

According to the BBC, I am a key figure in the extermination of the Jews, who will one day be called to give an account of my wickedness.

OTTER

How did they get your name?

KURT

Who knows?

OTTER

So you listen to the BBC?

KURT

I was informed my name had reached their hallowed list of infamy through the Ministry and the Reich's official listeners. It was almost like I was to be congratulated.

> OTTER looks around to be certain no one else is within hearing distance.

OTTER

But don't you see this as confirming the success of your charade?

KURT

I see this as making my struggle more difficult. I already knew of my success within the Ministry of Hygiene. In fact, I'm confident another promotion is eminent. This broadcast only gives the allies an excuse to disregard my voice.

OTTER

Don't tell me you think you must inform the English of their mistake?

KURT

It's essential.

    OTTER moves away.

OTTER

That is beyond my scope of capability. If my superiors won't run with your previous warning, they won't lift a finger to exonerate your reputation.

KURT

But please, try to—

OTTER

What about your influential friends in Helsinki?

    KURT pauses.

KURT

A great idea. I will go see the Director of Finnish Waterways—he has many contacts in Great Britain.

OTTER

And where is he, in Berlin?

KURT

No, no, no. He's headquartered in Helsinki.

OTTER

So you can just hop on a plane to Finland, is that it?

KURT

No problem. I will just order an assistant to requisition a plane in the name of Reichsführer Himmler—

OTTER

What?

KURT

Using forged papers, of course.

OTTER

Who would go along with such an order?

KURT

No problem at all. I have surrounded myself with former friends and youth group members who I've brought into the SS fold to cover my tracks and assist with the—to use your word—charade.

OTTER

All under the authority of Himmler's forged signature?

KURT

Yes.

> OTTER, shaking his head, looks intently at KURT.
> A PAUSE.

OTTER

Have a happy flight, Lieutenant Gerstein, a happy flight as you save the world and deliver you name from defamation.

> LIGHTS FALL on scene.
> The STAGE is DARK during EXTENDED PAUSE.

SLIDE SIXTEEN: Reichsführer Heinrich Himmler, supreme head of the SS

Act Two

> The LIGHTS COME UP on KURT standing at attention. HE does not move while HIMMLER speaks. HIMMLER is pacing back and forth behind KURT.

HIMMLER

You dare forge my name for a plane ride! I should have you shot right now!

> HIMMLER paces for a moment, continues to size up KURT.

HIMMLER (cont'd)

On your way to Finland, the plane had some mechanical difficulties forcing you to abort the flight and land in Riga. Now, of course, the officials at the Riga airport assume that I am on board. Understandably, an official welcoming committee lined up along the landing strip to welcome me. But I wasn't there, was I? Only you emerged. Instead of Heinrich Himmler, the natives of Riga get the one and only Kurt Gerstein. Naturally disappointed and more than a bit surprised, they phone Berlin, which brings you here.

> HIMMLER paces some more, walking around KURT, trying to size him up.

HIMMLER (cont'd)

Up to this incident, you have served the Reich, as I read in your file, with valor and intelligence. I have even heard of your impassioned writings to Germany's youth on the importance of moral and sexual purity.

> A PAUSE. HIMMLER just stares at KURT.

HIMMLER (cont'd)

And now to your story I am asked to believe, a story confirmed by your superior at the Ministry of Hygiene, Joachim Mrugowsky. You had to go to Finland, Lieutenant Gerstein, because the problem of drinking water in that country was becoming extremely serious. The rivers were heavily polluted with dead bodies. You had worked out a scientific solution to the problem and had taken the liberty of

HIMMLER (cont'd)
borrowing a plane in order to avoid bureaucratic delays and put the plan in action as soon as possible.

    HIMMLER paces, continues to size up KURT.

HIMMLER (cont'd)
You expect me to swallow this?

    A PAUSE. KURT is unsure of whether to answer.

HIMMLER (cont'd)
Answer the question.

KURT
    (After clearing his throat)
Yes.

HIMMLER
Really?

KURT
It is the truth, sir.

HIMMLER
If you needed to forge a signature, why not someone less conspicuous, like your chief, Mrugowsky?

KURT
The only name within the SS that would have hastened the delivery of the plane was yours, sir.

HIMMLER
And our Führer's, of course.

KURT
Yes, yes, of course.

    HIMMLER paces, continues to look KURT over.

HIMMLER

I respect audacity, even foolishness, in the name of zeal for the Reich. Adolf Hitler has enough minions who solve problems by consulting their rulebook first. You appear to consult your own mind, if not your conscience, first.

A PAUSE.

HIMMLER (cont'd)

You're an audacious fool, but to win this war we need more fools like you, Lieutenant Kurt Gerstein. And here is my decision on your fate. You will be forbidden to wear your uniform for a period of three weeks. The uniform represents a discipline and order that you have conveniently neglected. However it is a discipline and order that must reenlist your service after that time. Finally, you must not leave the country without Chief Mrugowsky's written permission. You are dismissed.

KURT starts to exit.

HIMMLER (cont'd)

Lieutenant Gerstein, one more thing before you leave.

KURT stops and turns to HIMMLER at attention.

HIMMLER (cont'd)

After we have won this war, you and I must discuss the great moral and religious problems of a post-war Europe.

KURT

Yes, sir. Heil Hitler!

HIMMLER

Heil Hitler.

The LIGHTS FADE on HIMMLER

SK

By the end of 1943 all the death camps using diesel gases were closed—Belzec in the autumn of 1942.

REGINA

The gas chambers were demolished. The mass graves dug up and the bodies drenched in oil and burnt on huge grills made from railway lines.

SK

But the work continued normally at camps like Auschwitz—where the chemical Zyklon B arose victorious to be the death agent of choice. Kurt Gerstein was assigned to secure the deliveries of such poisons posing as decontaminates, with only the occasional successful sabotage. But much was successfully delivered to the camps. Only so many accidents could be staged.

REGINA

And his hair was turning whiter and his face like that of a ghost. Perhaps preparing for the end, Gerstein sought to see his aged father.

> LIGHTS UP on another part of STAGE. KURT and HIS father, LUDWIG, sitting on park bench.
>
> REGINA is standing UPSTAGE, unseen by KURT and HIS father. SHE does not move, only listens, in the dark.

KURT

"I was greatly shocked by something you said, or rather wrote, to me at a difficult period in my life, when I was wrestling with problems of the utmost gravity."

LUDWIG

When weren't you wrestling with problems of the utmost gravity? To you life seemed to be a—

KURT

You told me "hard times call for hard measures."

LUDWIG

That is true—what is so shocking about the truth?

KURT

No! Such sentiment is an invitation to avoid self-examination.

LUDWIG

What?!

KURT

Such sentiment cannot justify the things that have gone on in Germany!

LUDWIG

Hard times call for hard measures!

KURT

I cannot believe, in light of so many outrageous events, that this is the last word of my father!

LUDWIG

You must quiet down, you are causing a disturbance.

    A PAUSE.

LUDWIG (cont'd)

And since when have you been concerned about anything I say?

    LUDWIG gets up from the bench.

LUDWIG (cont'd)

And this is what you called me for? I was hoping for reconciliation with a son who does not act like a son.

KURT

    (Quietly)
Do not go, please!

LUDWIG

Why should I not leave this disrespectful sermon? I am unrepentant; the march of history only requires the strong and determined to be willing to embrace the necessary measures of survival.

> KURT grabs HIS father's arm, not in anger, more in desperation.

KURT

But you must not be allowed to take such thoughts with you into the next world!

> LUDWIG pulls his arm away in disgust.

KURT (cont'd)

It seems to me that all of us who have still a little time to live will have sufficient reason to reflect on the practical possibilities and limitations—

LUDWIG

Hard times call for hard measures!

KURT

Does this allow for the casting away of all moral law? Does this excuse disregard for the image of God inherent in all people, including Jews?

LUDWIG

You "are a soldier and a servant of the State, and it is your business to obey your superiors. The responsibility lies with those who give the orders, not with those who execute them."

KURT

Then no one is culpable, since everyone is to some degree carrying out the orders of their superiors!

LUDWIG

No insubordination can be justified. You have simply to do what you are ordered to do!

KURT

Insufficient balm for a tortured conscience!

LUDWIG

I do not have a tortured conscience. Maybe someone else in Germany should, but I don't. You have simply to do what you are ordered to do. That, at least, is what I learnt as a servant of the State and a Prussian officer.

>   A PAUSE.

KURT

You have learnt well—sufficient to sleep soundly at night; sufficient to cast aside any self-doubts as the Allied bombs destroy houses around you. You have—

LUDWIG

Stop! I can see it was a mistake to try to reconcile—

KURT

We cannot and we must not win this war! The end is coming, Judge Gerstein!

LUDWIG

I have heard enough!

>   HE starts to exit.
>
>   KURT does not follow. HE at first speaks to HIS exited father, then, more frenzied, leaps as HIS passion dictates to greater volume and agitation as the following speech is hurled.

KURT

"We are deserving of a disastrous end, Father. The end of the regime in Germany must be something more than a matter of historical record—it must be an apocalyptic event. The outrage against Heaven could be expiated only in a calamity as monstrous and overwhelming as the offence itself, in the fiery reduction of Germany to dust and ashes, utter squalor, utter shame, so that the very sound of the word 'German' would cause Germans to regret that they had not been Jews!"

REGINA appears UPSTAGE.

REGINA

You might as well be howling at the moon. There is no one in the streets to hear you at this time of night.

> A PAUSE. KURT is briefly startled,

KURT

Maybe that is all there is left to do.

REGINA

What is that?

KURT

Howl at the moon.

> A PAUSE.

REGINA

(Not moving, softly)
You are pushing on things that will not move, Kurt Erich.

KURT

Consciences can't be moved?

REGINA

What do you expect from one who has already lived his life proudly—a death-bed confession?

KURT

The proud always take their excuses to the grave.

REGINA

And what of your excuses?

KURT

You mean the bromide, "I did what I could?"

REGINA
Yes.

KURT
I will go to my grave knowing they are filthy rags, filthy rags.

> The DIM LIGHTS further FADE.

SLIDE SEVENTEEN: On April 22, 1945, Kurt Gerstein surrendered to the French. Those that could testify as to the authenticity of his anti-Nazi espionage, his contacts in the various resistance movements and in the Confessing Church—especially Martin Niemöller—were all unable to be reached in time.

SLIDE EIGHTEEN: His testimony, therefore, was mostly disregarded by officials who could exonerate him. He would remain incarcerated as a war criminal.

SLIDE NINETEEN: Gerstein was taken to the Cherche-Midi Military Prison on July 5, 1945 and isolated in a small, dark, and lice-filled cell.

SLIDE TWENTY: On July 25, Kurt Gerstein was found dead in his cell, an apparent suicide.

THE END

www.ingramcontent.com/pod-product-compliance
Lightning Source LLC
Chambersburg PA
CBHW030454010526
44118CB00011B/927